MONTHLY

BILL TRACKER

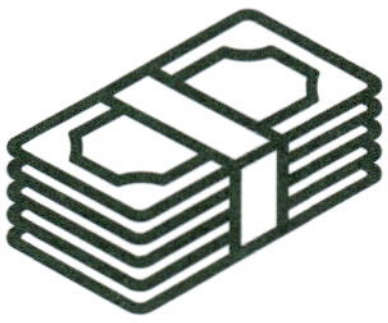

Organize and track
your monthly payments!

PETER PAUPER PRESS, INC.
RYE BROOK, NEW YORK

MONTH ....

MONTHLY BILL TRACKER

YEAR ....

PAID	BILL	DUE DATE	AMOUNT DUE	AMOUNT PAID	UNPAID BALANCE
☐					
☐					
☐					
☐					
☐					
☐					
☐					
☐					
☐					
☐					
☐					
☐					
☐					
☐					
☐					
☐					
☐					
☐					
☐					
☐					
☐					
☐					
☐					
☐					
☐					
☐					
☐					
		TOTAL			

NOTES

....

....

....

MONTH

MONTHLY BILL TRACKER

YEAR

PAID	BILL	DUE DATE	AMOUNT DUE	AMOUNT PAID	UNPAID BALANCE
☐					
☐					
☐					
☐					
☐					
☐					
☐					
☐					
☐					
☐					
☐					
☐					
☐					
☐					
☐					
☐					
☐					
☐					
☐					
☐					
☐					
☐					
☐					
☐					
☐					
☐					
☐					
		TOTAL			

NOTES

MONTH

MONTHLY BILL TRACKER

YEAR

PAID	BILL	DUE DATE	AMOUNT DUE	AMOUNT PAID	UNPAID BALANCE
☐					
☐					
☐					
☐					
☐					
☐					
☐					
☐					
☐					
☐					
☐					
☐					
☐					
☐					
☐					
☐					
☐					
☐					
☐					
☐					
☐					
☐					
☐					
☐					
☐					
☐					
☐					
		TOTAL			

NOTES

MONTH

MONTHLY BILL TRACKER

YEAR

PAID	BILL	DUE DATE	AMOUNT DUE	AMOUNT PAID	UNPAID BALANCE
☐					
☐					
☐					
☐					
☐					
☐					
☐					
☐					
☐					
☐					
☐					
☐					
☐					
☐					
☐					
☐					
☐					
☐					
☐					
☐					
☐					
☐					
☐					
☐					
☐					
☐					
☐					
		TOTAL			

NOTES

MONTH

MONTHLY BILL TRACKER

YEAR

PAID	BILL	DUE DATE	AMOUNT DUE	AMOUNT PAID	UNPAID BALANCE
☐					
☐					
☐					
☐					
☐					
☐					
☐					
☐					
☐					
☐					
☐					
☐					
☐					
☐					
☐					
☐					
☐					
☐					
☐					
☐					
☐					
☐					
☐					
☐					
☐					
☐					
		TOTAL			

NOTES

MONTH

MONTHLY BILL TRACKER

YEAR

PAID	BILL	DUE DATE	AMOUNT DUE	AMOUNT PAID	UNPAID BALANCE
☐					
☐					
☐					
☐					
☐					
☐					
☐					
☐					
☐					
☐					
☐					
☐					
☐					
☐					
☐					
☐					
☐					
☐					
☐					
☐					
☐					
☐					
☐					
☐					
☐					
☐					
☐					
		TOTAL			

NOTES

MONTH ....

MONTHLY BILL TRACKER

YEAR ....

PAID	BILL	DUE DATE	AMOUNT DUE	AMOUNT PAID	UNPAID BALANCE
☐					
☐					
☐					
☐					
☐					
☐					
☐					
☐					
☐					
☐					
☐					
☐					
☐					
☐					
☐					
☐					
☐					
☐					
☐					
☐					
☐					
☐					
☐					
☐					
☐					
☐					
☐					
		TOTAL			

NOTES

....

....

....

MONTH

MONTHLY BILL TRACKER

YEAR

PAID	BILL	DUE DATE	AMOUNT DUE	AMOUNT PAID	UNPAID BALANCE
☐					
☐					
☐					
☐					
☐					
☐					
☐					
☐					
☐					
☐					
☐					
☐					
☐					
☐					
☐					
☐					
☐					
☐					
☐					
☐					
☐					
☐					
☐					
☐					
☐					
☐					
☐					
		TOTAL			

NOTES

MONTH ....

MONTHLY BILL TRACKER

YEAR ....

PAID	BILL	DUE DATE	AMOUNT DUE	AMOUNT PAID	UNPAID BALANCE
☐					
☐					
☐					
☐					
☐					
☐					
☐					
☐					
☐					
☐					
☐					
☐					
☐					
☐					
☐					
☐					
☐					
☐					
☐					
☐					
☐					
☐					
☐					
☐					
☐					
☐					
		TOTAL			

NOTES

....

....

....

MONTH

MONTHLY BILL TRACKER

YEAR

PAID	BILL	DUE DATE	AMOUNT DUE	AMOUNT PAID	UNPAID BALANCE
☐					
☐					
☐					
☐					
☐					
☐					
☐					
☐					
☐					
☐					
☐					
☐					
☐					
☐					
☐					
☐					
☐					
☐					
☐					
☐					
☐					
☐					
☐					
☐					
☐					
☐					
		TOTAL			

NOTES

MONTH ....

MONTHLY BILL TRACKER

YEAR ....

PAID	BILL	DUE DATE	AMOUNT DUE	AMOUNT PAID	UNPAID BALANCE
☐					
☐					
☐					
☐					
☐					
☐					
☐					
☐					
☐					
☐					
☐					
☐					
☐					
☐					
☐					
☐					
☐					
☐					
☐					
☐					
☐					
☐					
☐					
☐					
☐					
☐					
☐					
		TOTAL			

NOTES

MONTH

MONTHLY BILL TRACKER

YEAR

PAID	BILL	DUE DATE	AMOUNT DUE	AMOUNT PAID	UNPAID BALANCE
☐					
☐					
☐					
☐					
☐					
☐					
☐					
☐					
☐					
☐					
☐					
☐					
☐					
☐					
☐					
☐					
☐					
☐					
☐					
☐					
☐					
☐					
☐					
☐					
☐					
☐					
☐					
		TOTAL			

NOTES

MONTH

MONTHLY BILL TRACKER

YEAR

PAID	BILL	DUE DATE	AMOUNT DUE	AMOUNT PAID	UNPAID BALANCE
☐					
☐					
☐					
☐					
☐					
☐					
☐					
☐					
☐					
☐					
☐					
☐					
☐					
☐					
☐					
☐					
☐					
☐					
☐					
☐					
☐					
☐					
☐					
☐					
☐					
☐					
☐					
		TOTAL			

NOTES

MONTH

MONTHLY BILL TRACKER

YEAR

PAID	BILL	DUE DATE	AMOUNT DUE	AMOUNT PAID	UNPAID BALANCE
☐					
☐					
☐					
☐					
☐					
☐					
☐					
☐					
☐					
☐					
☐					
☐					
☐					
☐					
☐					
☐					
☐					
☐					
☐					
☐					
☐					
☐					
☐					
☐					
☐					
☐					
☐					
		TOTAL			

NOTES

MONTH

MONTHLY BILL TRACKER

YEAR

PAID	BILL	DUE DATE	AMOUNT DUE	AMOUNT PAID	UNPAID BALANCE
☐					
☐					
☐					
☐					
☐					
☐					
☐					
☐					
☐					
☐					
☐					
☐					
☐					
☐					
☐					
☐					
☐					
☐					
☐					
☐					
☐					
☐					
☐					
☐					
☐					
☐					
☐					
		TOTAL			

NOTES

MONTH ....

MONTHLY BILL TRACKER

YEAR ....

PAID	BILL	DUE DATE	AMOUNT DUE	AMOUNT PAID	UNPAID BALANCE
☐					
☐					
☐					
☐					
☐					
☐					
☐					
☐					
☐					
☐					
☐					
☐					
☐					
☐					
☐					
☐					
☐					
☐					
☐					
☐					
☐					
☐					
☐					
☐					
☐					
☐					
		TOTAL			

NOTES

MONTH ....

MONTHLY BILL TRACKER

YEAR ....

PAID	BILL	DUE DATE	AMOUNT DUE	AMOUNT PAID	UNPAID BALANCE
☐					
☐					
☐					
☐					
☐					
☐					
☐					
☐					
☐					
☐					
☐					
☐					
☐					
☐					
☐					
☐					
☐					
☐					
☐					
☐					
☐					
☐					
☐					
☐					
☐					
☐					
☐					
		TOTAL			

NOTES

MONTH

MONTHLY BILL TRACKER

YEAR

PAID	BILL	DUE DATE	AMOUNT DUE	AMOUNT PAID	UNPAID BALANCE
☐					
☐					
☐					
☐					
☐					
☐					
☐					
☐					
☐					
☐					
☐					
☐					
☐					
☐					
☐					
☐					
☐					
☐					
☐					
☐					
☐					
☐					
☐					
☐					
☐					
☐					
☐					
		TOTAL			

NOTES

MONTH

MONTHLY BILL TRACKER

YEAR

PAID	BILL	DUE DATE	AMOUNT DUE	AMOUNT PAID	UNPAID BALANCE
☐					
☐					
☐					
☐					
☐					
☐					
☐					
☐					
☐					
☐					
☐					
☐					
☐					
☐					
☐					
☐					
☐					
☐					
☐					
☐					
☐					
☐					
☐					
☐					
☐					
☐					
☐					
		TOTAL			

NOTES

MONTH

MONTHLY BILL TRACKER

YEAR

PAID	BILL	DUE DATE	AMOUNT DUE	AMOUNT PAID	UNPAID BALANCE
☐					
☐					
☐					
☐					
☐					
☐					
☐					
☐					
☐					
☐					
☐					
☐					
☐					
☐					
☐					
☐					
☐					
☐					
☐					
☐					
☐					
☐					
☐					
☐					
☐					
☐					
☐					
		TOTAL			

NOTES

MONTH

MONTHLY BILL TRACKER

YEAR

PAID	BILL	DUE DATE	AMOUNT DUE	AMOUNT PAID	UNPAID BALANCE
☐					
☐					
☐					
☐					
☐					
☐					
☐					
☐					
☐					
☐					
☐					
☐					
☐					
☐					
☐					
☐					
☐					
☐					
☐					
☐					
☐					
☐					
☐					
☐					
☐					
☐					
☐					
		TOTAL			

NOTES

MONTH ....

MONTHLY BILL TRACKER

YEAR ....

PAID	BILL	DUE DATE	AMOUNT DUE	AMOUNT PAID	UNPAID BALANCE
☐					
☐					
☐					
☐					
☐					
☐					
☐					
☐					
☐					
☐					
☐					
☐					
☐					
☐					
☐					
☐					
☐					
☐					
☐					
☐					
☐					
☐					
☐					
☐					
☐					
☐					
☐					
		TOTAL			

NOTES

....

....

....

MONTH ....

MONTHLY BILL TRACKER

YEAR ....

PAID	BILL	DUE DATE	AMOUNT DUE	AMOUNT PAID	UNPAID BALANCE
☐					
☐					
☐					
☐					
☐					
☐					
☐					
☐					
☐					
☐					
☐					
☐					
☐					
☐					
☐					
☐					
☐					
☐					
☐					
☐					
☐					
☐					
☐					
☐					
☐					
☐					
☐					
		TOTAL			

NOTES

....

....

....

MONTH

MONTHLY BILL TRACKER

YEAR

PAID	BILL	DUE DATE	AMOUNT DUE	AMOUNT PAID	UNPAID BALANCE
☐					
☐					
☐					
☐					
☐					
☐					
☐					
☐					
☐					
☐					
☐					
☐					
☐					
☐					
☐					
☐					
☐					
☐					
☐					
☐					
☐					
☐					
☐					
☐					
☐					
☐					
☐					
		TOTAL			

NOTES

MONTH ....

MONTHLY BILL TRACKER

YEAR ....

PAID	BILL	DUE DATE	AMOUNT DUE	AMOUNT PAID	UNPAID BALANCE
☐					
☐					
☐					
☐					
☐					
☐					
☐					
☐					
☐					
☐					
☐					
☐					
☐					
☐					
☐					
☐					
☐					
☐					
☐					
☐					
☐					
☐					
☐					
☐					
☐					
☐					
☐					
		TOTAL			

NOTES

MONTH

MONTHLY BILL TRACKER

YEAR

PAID	BILL	DUE DATE	AMOUNT DUE	AMOUNT PAID	UNPAID BALANCE
☐					
☐					
☐					
☐					
☐					
☐					
☐					
☐					
☐					
☐					
☐					
☐					
☐					
☐					
☐					
☐					
☐					
☐					
☐					
☐					
☐					
☐					
☐					
☐					
☐					
☐					
☐					
		TOTAL			

NOTES

MONTH ....

MONTHLY BILL TRACKER

YEAR ....

PAID	BILL	DUE DATE	AMOUNT DUE	AMOUNT PAID	UNPAID BALANCE
☐					
☐					
☐					
☐					
☐					
☐					
☐					
☐					
☐					
☐					
☐					
☐					
☐					
☐					
☐					
☐					
☐					
☐					
☐					
☐					
☐					
☐					
☐					
☐					
☐					
☐					
☐					
		TOTAL			

NOTES

MONTH

MONTHLY BILL TRACKER

YEAR

PAID	BILL	DUE DATE	AMOUNT DUE	AMOUNT PAID	UNPAID BALANCE
☐					
☐					
☐					
☐					
☐					
☐					
☐					
☐					
☐					
☐					
☐					
☐					
☐					
☐					
☐					
☐					
☐					
☐					
☐					
☐					
☐					
☐					
☐					
☐					
☐					
☐					
☐					
		TOTAL			

NOTES

MONTH

MONTHLY BILL TRACKER

YEAR

PAID	BILL	DUE DATE	AMOUNT DUE	AMOUNT PAID	UNPAID BALANCE
☐					
☐					
☐					
☐					
☐					
☐					
☐					
☐					
☐					
☐					
☐					
☐					
☐					
☐					
☐					
☐					
☐					
☐					
☐					
☐					
☐					
☐					
☐					
☐					
☐					
☐					
		TOTAL			

NOTES

MONTH

MONTHLY BILL TRACKER

YEAR

PAID	BILL	DUE DATE	AMOUNT DUE	AMOUNT PAID	UNPAID BALANCE
☐					
☐					
☐					
☐					
☐					
☐					
☐					
☐					
☐					
☐					
☐					
☐					
☐					
☐					
☐					
☐					
☐					
☐					
☐					
☐					
☐					
☐					
☐					
☐					
☐					
☐					
		TOTAL			

NOTES

MONTH

MONTHLY BILL TRACKER

YEAR

PAID	BILL	DUE DATE	AMOUNT DUE	AMOUNT PAID	UNPAID BALANCE
☐					
☐					
☐					
☐					
☐					
☐					
☐					
☐					
☐					
☐					
☐					
☐					
☐					
☐					
☐					
☐					
☐					
☐					
☐					
☐					
☐					
☐					
☐					
☐					
☐					
☐					
☐					
		TOTAL			

NOTES

MONTH

MONTHLY BILL TRACKER

YEAR

PAID	BILL	DUE DATE	AMOUNT DUE	AMOUNT PAID	UNPAID BALANCE
☐					
☐					
☐					
☐					
☐					
☐					
☐					
☐					
☐					
☐					
☐					
☐					
☐					
☐					
☐					
☐					
☐					
☐					
☐					
☐					
☐					
☐					
☐					
☐					
☐					
☐					
☐					
		TOTAL			

NOTES

MONTH

MONTHLY BILL TRACKER

YEAR

PAID	BILL	DUE DATE	AMOUNT DUE	AMOUNT PAID	UNPAID BALANCE
☐					
☐					
☐					
☐					
☐					
☐					
☐					
☐					
☐					
☐					
☐					
☐					
☐					
☐					
☐					
☐					
☐					
☐					
☐					
☐					
☐					
☐					
☐					
☐					
☐					
☐					
☐					
		TOTAL			

NOTES

MONTH

MONTHLY BILL TRACKER

YEAR

PAID	BILL	DUE DATE	AMOUNT DUE	AMOUNT PAID	UNPAID BALANCE
☐					
☐					
☐					
☐					
☐					
☐					
☐					
☐					
☐					
☐					
☐					
☐					
☐					
☐					
☐					
☐					
☐					
☐					
☐					
☐					
☐					
☐					
☐					
☐					
☐					
☐					
☐					
		TOTAL			

NOTES

MONTH ....

MONTHLY BILL TRACKER

YEAR ....

PAID	BILL	DUE DATE	AMOUNT DUE	AMOUNT PAID	UNPAID BALANCE
☐					
☐					
☐					
☐					
☐					
☐					
☐					
☐					
☐					
☐					
☐					
☐					
☐					
☐					
☐					
☐					
☐					
☐					
☐					
☐					
☐					
☐					
☐					
☐					
☐					
☐					
☐					
		TOTAL			

NOTES

MONTH

MONTHLY BILL TRACKER

YEAR

PAID	BILL	DUE DATE	AMOUNT DUE	AMOUNT PAID	UNPAID BALANCE
☐					
☐					
☐					
☐					
☐					
☐					
☐					
☐					
☐					
☐					
☐					
☐					
☐					
☐					
☐					
☐					
☐					
☐					
☐					
☐					
☐					
☐					
☐					
☐					
☐					
☐					
☐					
		TOTAL			

NOTES

MONTH ....

MONTHLY BILL TRACKER

YEAR ....

PAID	BILL	DUE DATE	AMOUNT DUE	AMOUNT PAID	UNPAID BALANCE
☐					
☐					
☐					
☐					
☐					
☐					
☐					
☐					
☐					
☐					
☐					
☐					
☐					
☐					
☐					
☐					
☐					
☐					
☐					
☐					
☐					
☐					
☐					
☐					
☐					
☐					
☐					
		TOTAL			

NOTES

MONTH ....

MONTHLY BILL TRACKER

YEAR ....

PAID	BILL	DUE DATE	AMOUNT DUE	AMOUNT PAID	UNPAID BALANCE
☐					
☐					
☐					
☐					
☐					
☐					
☐					
☐					
☐					
☐					
☐					
☐					
☐					
☐					
☐					
☐					
☐					
☐					
☐					
☐					
☐					
☐					
☐					
☐					
☐					
☐					
☐					
		TOTAL			

NOTES

MONTH

MONTHLY BILL TRACKER

YEAR

PAID	BILL	DUE DATE	AMOUNT DUE	AMOUNT PAID	UNPAID BALANCE
☐					
☐					
☐					
☐					
☐					
☐					
☐					
☐					
☐					
☐					
☐					
☐					
☐					
☐					
☐					
☐					
☐					
☐					
☐					
☐					
☐					
☐					
☐					
☐					
☐					
☐					
		TOTAL			

NOTES

MONTH

MONTHLY BILL TRACKER

YEAR

PAID	BILL	DUE DATE	AMOUNT DUE	AMOUNT PAID	UNPAID BALANCE
☐					
☐					
☐					
☐					
☐					
☐					
☐					
☐					
☐					
☐					
☐					
☐					
☐					
☐					
☐					
☐					
☐					
☐					
☐					
☐					
☐					
☐					
☐					
☐					
☐					
☐					
☐					
		TOTAL			

NOTES

MONTH

MONTHLY BILL TRACKER

YEAR

PAID	BILL	DUE DATE	AMOUNT DUE	AMOUNT PAID	UNPAID BALANCE
☐					
☐					
☐					
☐					
☐					
☐					
☐					
☐					
☐					
☐					
☐					
☐					
☐					
☐					
☐					
☐					
☐					
☐					
☐					
☐					
☐					
☐					
☐					
☐					
☐					
☐					
☐					
		TOTAL			

NOTES

MONTHLY BILL TRACKER

MONTH .... YEAR ....

PAID	BILL	DUE DATE	AMOUNT DUE	AMOUNT PAID	UNPAID BALANCE
☐					
☐					
☐					
☐					
☐					
☐					
☐					
☐					
☐					
☐					
☐					
☐					
☐					
☐					
☐					
☐					
☐					
☐					
☐					
☐					
☐					
☐					
☐					
☐					
☐					
☐					
☐					
		TOTAL			

NOTES

MONTH

MONTHLY BILL TRACKER

YEAR

PAID	BILL	DUE DATE	AMOUNT DUE	AMOUNT PAID	UNPAID BALANCE
☐					
☐					
☐					
☐					
☐					
☐					
☐					
☐					
☐					
☐					
☐					
☐					
☐					
☐					
☐					
☐					
☐					
☐					
☐					
☐					
☐					
☐					
☐					
☐					
☐					
☐					
☐					
		TOTAL			

NOTES

MONTH

MONTHLY BILL TRACKER

YEAR

PAID	BILL	DUE DATE	AMOUNT DUE	AMOUNT PAID	UNPAID BALANCE
☐					
☐					
☐					
☐					
☐					
☐					
☐					
☐					
☐					
☐					
☐					
☐					
☐					
☐					
☐					
☐					
☐					
☐					
☐					
☐					
☐					
☐					
☐					
☐					
☐					
☐					
☐					
		TOTAL			

NOTES

MONTH

MONTHLY BILL TRACKER

YEAR

PAID	BILL	DUE DATE	AMOUNT DUE	AMOUNT PAID	UNPAID BALANCE
☐					
☐					
☐					
☐					
☐					
☐					
☐					
☐					
☐					
☐					
☐					
☐					
☐					
☐					
☐					
☐					
☐					
☐					
☐					
☐					
☐					
☐					
☐					
☐					
☐					
☐					
☐					
		TOTAL			

NOTES

MONTH ....

MONTHLY BILL TRACKER

YEAR ....

PAID	BILL	DUE DATE	AMOUNT DUE	AMOUNT PAID	UNPAID BALANCE
☐					
☐					
☐					
☐					
☐					
☐					
☐					
☐					
☐					
☐					
☐					
☐					
☐					
☐					
☐					
☐					
☐					
☐					
☐					
☐					
☐					
☐					
☐					
☐					
☐					
☐					
		TOTAL			

NOTES

MONTH

MONTHLY BILL TRACKER

YEAR

PAID	BILL	DUE DATE	AMOUNT DUE	AMOUNT PAID	UNPAID BALANCE
☐					
☐					
☐					
☐					
☐					
☐					
☐					
☐					
☐					
☐					
☐					
☐					
☐					
☐					
☐					
☐					
☐					
☐					
☐					
☐					
☐					
☐					
☐					
☐					
☐					
☐					
☐					
		TOTAL			

NOTES

MONTH

MONTHLY BILL TRACKER

YEAR

PAID	BILL	DUE DATE	AMOUNT DUE	AMOUNT PAID	UNPAID BALANCE
☐					
☐					
☐					
☐					
☐					
☐					
☐					
☐					
☐					
☐					
☐					
☐					
☐					
☐					
☐					
☐					
☐					
☐					
☐					
☐					
☐					
☐					
☐					
☐					
☐					
☐					
☐					
		TOTAL			

NOTES

MONTH

MONTHLY BILL TRACKER

YEAR

PAID	BILL	DUE DATE	AMOUNT DUE	AMOUNT PAID	UNPAID BALANCE
☐					
☐					
☐					
☐					
☐					
☐					
☐					
☐					
☐					
☐					
☐					
☐					
☐					
☐					
☐					
☐					
☐					
☐					
☐					
☐					
☐					
☐					
☐					
☐					
☐					
☐					
☐					
		TOTAL			

NOTES

MONTH

MONTHLY BILL TRACKER

YEAR

PAID	BILL	DUE DATE	AMOUNT DUE	AMOUNT PAID	UNPAID BALANCE
☐					
☐					
☐					
☐					
☐					
☐					
☐					
☐					
☐					
☐					
☐					
☐					
☐					
☐					
☐					
☐					
☐					
☐					
☐					
☐					
☐					
☐					
☐					
☐					
☐					
☐					
☐					
		TOTAL			

NOTES

MONTH ....

MONTHLY BILL TRACKER

YEAR ....

PAID	BILL	DUE DATE	AMOUNT DUE	AMOUNT PAID	UNPAID BALANCE
☐					
☐					
☐					
☐					
☐					
☐					
☐					
☐					
☐					
☐					
☐					
☐					
☐					
☐					
☐					
☐					
☐					
☐					
☐					
☐					
☐					
☐					
☐					
☐					
☐					
☐					
☐					
		TOTAL			

NOTES

MONTH

MONTHLY BILL TRACKER

YEAR

PAID	BILL	DUE DATE	AMOUNT DUE	AMOUNT PAID	UNPAID BALANCE
☐					
☐					
☐					
☐					
☐					
☐					
☐					
☐					
☐					
☐					
☐					
☐					
☐					
☐					
☐					
☐					
☐					
☐					
☐					
☐					
☐					
☐					
☐					
☐					
☐					
☐					
		TOTAL			

NOTES

MONTH

MONTHLY BILL TRACKER

YEAR

PAID	BILL	DUE DATE	AMOUNT DUE	AMOUNT PAID	UNPAID BALANCE
☐					
☐					
☐					
☐					
☐					
☐					
☐					
☐					
☐					
☐					
☐					
☐					
☐					
☐					
☐					
☐					
☐					
☐					
☐					
☐					
☐					
☐					
☐					
☐					
☐					
☐					
☐					
		TOTAL			

NOTES

MONTH ....

MONTHLY BILL TRACKER

YEAR ....

PAID	BILL	DUE DATE	AMOUNT DUE	AMOUNT PAID	UNPAID BALANCE
☐					
☐					
☐					
☐					
☐					
☐					
☐					
☐					
☐					
☐					
☐					
☐					
☐					
☐					
☐					
☐					
☐					
☐					
☐					
☐					
☐					
☐					
☐					
☐					
☐					
☐					
☐					
		TOTAL			

NOTES

MONTH

MONTHLY BILL TRACKER

YEAR

PAID	BILL	DUE DATE	AMOUNT DUE	AMOUNT PAID	UNPAID BALANCE
☐					
☐					
☐					
☐					
☐					
☐					
☐					
☐					
☐					
☐					
☐					
☐					
☐					
☐					
☐					
☐					
☐					
☐					
☐					
☐					
☐					
☐					
☐					
☐					
☐					
☐					
☐					
		TOTAL			

NOTES

MONTH ....

MONTHLY BILL TRACKER

YEAR ....

PAID	BILL	DUE DATE	AMOUNT DUE	AMOUNT PAID	UNPAID BALANCE
☐					
☐					
☐					
☐					
☐					
☐					
☐					
☐					
☐					
☐					
☐					
☐					
☐					
☐					
☐					
☐					
☐					
☐					
☐					
☐					
☐					
☐					
☐					
☐					
☐					
☐					
☐					
		TOTAL			

NOTES

MONTH ....

MONTHLY BILL TRACKER

YEAR ....

PAID	BILL	DUE DATE	AMOUNT DUE	AMOUNT PAID	UNPAID BALANCE
☐					
☐					
☐					
☐					
☐					
☐					
☐					
☐					
☐					
☐					
☐					
☐					
☐					
☐					
☐					
☐					
☐					
☐					
☐					
☐					
☐					
☐					
☐					
☐					
☐					
☐					
☐					
		TOTAL			

NOTES

MONTH ....

MONTHLY BILL TRACKER

YEAR ....

PAID	BILL	DUE DATE	AMOUNT DUE	AMOUNT PAID	UNPAID BALANCE
☐					
☐					
☐					
☐					
☐					
☐					
☐					
☐					
☐					
☐					
☐					
☐					
☐					
☐					
☐					
☐					
☐					
☐					
☐					
☐					
☐					
☐					
☐					
☐					
☐					
☐					
☐					
		TOTAL			

NOTES

MONTH ....

MONTHLY BILL TRACKER

YEAR ....

PAID	BILL	DUE DATE	AMOUNT DUE	AMOUNT PAID	UNPAID BALANCE
☐					
☐					
☐					
☐					
☐					
☐					
☐					
☐					
☐					
☐					
☐					
☐					
☐					
☐					
☐					
☐					
☐					
☐					
☐					
☐					
☐					
☐					
☐					
☐					
☐					
☐					
☐					
		TOTAL			

NOTES

MONTH

MONTHLY BILL TRACKER

YEAR

PAID	BILL	DUE DATE	AMOUNT DUE	AMOUNT PAID	UNPAID BALANCE
☐					
☐					
☐					
☐					
☐					
☐					
☐					
☐					
☐					
☐					
☐					
☐					
☐					
☐					
☐					
☐					
☐					
☐					
☐					
☐					
☐					
☐					
☐					
☐					
☐					
☐					
		TOTAL			

NOTES

MONTH

MONTHLY BILL TRACKER

YEAR

PAID	BILL	DUE DATE	AMOUNT DUE	AMOUNT PAID	UNPAID BALANCE
☐					
☐					
☐					
☐					
☐					
☐					
☐					
☐					
☐					
☐					
☐					
☐					
☐					
☐					
☐					
☐					
☐					
☐					
☐					
☐					
☐					
☐					
☐					
☐					
☐					
☐					
		TOTAL			

NOTES

MONTH .... **MONTHLY BILL TRACKER** YEAR ....

PAID	BILL	DUE DATE	AMOUNT DUE	AMOUNT PAID	UNPAID BALANCE
☐					
☐					
☐					
☐					
☐					
☐					
☐					
☐					
☐					
☐					
☐					
☐					
☐					
☐					
☐					
☐					
☐					
☐					
☐					
☐					
☐					
☐					
☐					
☐					
☐					
☐					
☐					
		TOTAL			

NOTES

....

....

....

MONTH

MONTHLY BILL TRACKER

YEAR

PAID	BILL	DUE DATE	AMOUNT DUE	AMOUNT PAID	UNPAID BALANCE
☐					
☐					
☐					
☐					
☐					
☐					
☐					
☐					
☐					
☐					
☐					
☐					
☐					
☐					
☐					
☐					
☐					
☐					
☐					
☐					
☐					
☐					
☐					
☐					
☐					
☐					
☐					
		TOTAL			

NOTES

MONTH ....

MONTHLY BILL TRACKER

YEAR ....

PAID	BILL	DUE DATE	AMOUNT DUE	AMOUNT PAID	UNPAID BALANCE
☐					
☐					
☐					
☐					
☐					
☐					
☐					
☐					
☐					
☐					
☐					
☐					
☐					
☐					
☐					
☐					
☐					
☐					
☐					
☐					
☐					
☐					
☐					
☐					
☐					
☐					
☐					
		TOTAL			

NOTES

....

....

....

MONTH

MONTHLY BILL TRACKER

YEAR

PAID	BILL	DUE DATE	AMOUNT DUE	AMOUNT PAID	UNPAID BALANCE
☐					
☐					
☐					
☐					
☐					
☐					
☐					
☐					
☐					
☐					
☐					
☐					
☐					
☐					
☐					
☐					
☐					
☐					
☐					
☐					
☐					
☐					
☐					
☐					
☐					
☐					
☐					
		TOTAL			

NOTES

MONTH ....

MONTHLY BILL TRACKER

YEAR ....

PAID	BILL	DUE DATE	AMOUNT DUE	AMOUNT PAID	UNPAID BALANCE
☐					
☐					
☐					
☐					
☐					
☐					
☐					
☐					
☐					
☐					
☐					
☐					
☐					
☐					
☐					
☐					
☐					
☐					
☐					
☐					
☐					
☐					
☐					
☐					
☐					
☐					
		TOTAL			

NOTES

MONTHLY BILL TRACKER

MONTH ....

YEAR ....

PAID	BILL	DUE DATE	AMOUNT DUE	AMOUNT PAID	UNPAID BALANCE
☐					
☐					
☐					
☐					
☐					
☐					
☐					
☐					
☐					
☐					
☐					
☐					
☐					
☐					
☐					
☐					
☐					
☐					
☐					
☐					
☐					
☐					
☐					
☐					
☐					
☐					
☐					
		TOTAL			

NOTES

MONTH

MONTHLY BILL TRACKER

YEAR

PAID	BILL	DUE DATE	AMOUNT DUE	AMOUNT PAID	UNPAID BALANCE
☐					
☐					
☐					
☐					
☐					
☐					
☐					
☐					
☐					
☐					
☐					
☐					
☐					
☐					
☐					
☐					
☐					
☐					
☐					
☐					
☐					
☐					
☐					
☐					
☐					
☐					
☐					
		TOTAL			

NOTES

MONTH

MONTHLY BILL TRACKER

YEAR

PAID	BILL	DUE DATE	AMOUNT DUE	AMOUNT PAID	UNPAID BALANCE
☐					
☐					
☐					
☐					
☐					
☐					
☐					
☐					
☐					
☐					
☐					
☐					
☐					
☐					
☐					
☐					
☐					
☐					
☐					
☐					
☐					
☐					
☐					
☐					
☐					
☐					
☐					
		TOTAL			

NOTES

MONTH

MONTHLY BILL TRACKER

YEAR

PAID	BILL	DUE DATE	AMOUNT DUE	AMOUNT PAID	UNPAID BALANCE
☐					
☐					
☐					
☐					
☐					
☐					
☐					
☐					
☐					
☐					
☐					
☐					
☐					
☐					
☐					
☐					
☐					
☐					
☐					
☐					
☐					
☐					
☐					
☐					
☐					
☐					
☐					
		TOTAL			

NOTES

MONTH ....

MONTHLY BILL TRACKER

YEAR ....

PAID	BILL	DUE DATE	AMOUNT DUE	AMOUNT PAID	UNPAID BALANCE
☐					
☐					
☐					
☐					
☐					
☐					
☐					
☐					
☐					
☐					
☐					
☐					
☐					
☐					
☐					
☐					
☐					
☐					
☐					
☐					
☐					
☐					
☐					
☐					
☐					
☐					
		TOTAL			

NOTES

MONTH

MONTHLY BILL TRACKER

YEAR

PAID	BILL	DUE DATE	AMOUNT DUE	AMOUNT PAID	UNPAID BALANCE
☐					
☐					
☐					
☐					
☐					
☐					
☐					
☐					
☐					
☐					
☐					
☐					
☐					
☐					
☐					
☐					
☐					
☐					
☐					
☐					
☐					
☐					
☐					
☐					
☐					
☐					
		TOTAL			

NOTES

MONTH

MONTHLY BILL TRACKER

YEAR

PAID	BILL	DUE DATE	AMOUNT DUE	AMOUNT PAID	UNPAID BALANCE
☐					
☐					
☐					
☐					
☐					
☐					
☐					
☐					
☐					
☐					
☐					
☐					
☐					
☐					
☐					
☐					
☐					
☐					
☐					
☐					
☐					
☐					
☐					
☐					
☐					
☐					
☐					
		TOTAL			

NOTES

MONTH

MONTHLY BILL TRACKER

YEAR

PAID	BILL	DUE DATE	AMOUNT DUE	AMOUNT PAID	UNPAID BALANCE
☐					
☐					
☐					
☐					
☐					
☐					
☐					
☐					
☐					
☐					
☐					
☐					
☐					
☐					
☐					
☐					
☐					
☐					
☐					
☐					
☐					
☐					
☐					
☐					
☐					
☐					
☐					
	TOTAL				

NOTES

MONTH

MONTHLY BILL TRACKER

YEAR

PAID	BILL	DUE DATE	AMOUNT DUE	AMOUNT PAID	UNPAID BALANCE
☐					
☐					
☐					
☐					
☐					
☐					
☐					
☐					
☐					
☐					
☐					
☐					
☐					
☐					
☐					
☐					
☐					
☐					
☐					
☐					
☐					
☐					
☐					
☐					
☐					
☐					
		TOTAL			

NOTES

MONTH

MONTHLY BILL TRACKER

YEAR

PAID	BILL	DUE DATE	AMOUNT DUE	AMOUNT PAID	UNPAID BALANCE
☐					
☐					
☐					
☐					
☐					
☐					
☐					
☐					
☐					
☐					
☐					
☐					
☐					
☐					
☐					
☐					
☐					
☐					
☐					
☐					
☐					
☐					
☐					
☐					
☐					
☐					
☐					
		TOTAL			

NOTES

MONTH

MONTHLY BILL TRACKER

YEAR

PAID	BILL	DUE DATE	AMOUNT DUE	AMOUNT PAID	UNPAID BALANCE
☐					
☐					
☐					
☐					
☐					
☐					
☐					
☐					
☐					
☐					
☐					
☐					
☐					
☐					
☐					
☐					
☐					
☐					
☐					
☐					
☐					
☐					
☐					
☐					
☐					
☐					
☐					
		TOTAL			

NOTES

MONTH

MONTHLY BILL TRACKER

YEAR

PAID	BILL	DUE DATE	AMOUNT DUE	AMOUNT PAID	UNPAID BALANCE
☐					
☐					
☐					
☐					
☐					
☐					
☐					
☐					
☐					
☐					
☐					
☐					
☐					
☐					
☐					
☐					
☐					
☐					
☐					
☐					
☐					
☐					
☐					
☐					
☐					
☐					
☐					
		TOTAL			

NOTES

MONTH ....

MONTHLY BILL TRACKER

YEAR ....

PAID	BILL	DUE DATE	AMOUNT DUE	AMOUNT PAID	UNPAID BALANCE
☐					
☐					
☐					
☐					
☐					
☐					
☐					
☐					
☐					
☐					
☐					
☐					
☐					
☐					
☐					
☐					
☐					
☐					
☐					
☐					
☐					
☐					
☐					
☐					
☐					
☐					
☐					
		TOTAL			

NOTES

....

....

....

MONTH ....

MONTHLY BILL TRACKER

YEAR ....

PAID	BILL	DUE DATE	AMOUNT DUE	AMOUNT PAID	UNPAID BALANCE
☐					
☐					
☐					
☐					
☐					
☐					
☐					
☐					
☐					
☐					
☐					
☐					
☐					
☐					
☐					
☐					
☐					
☐					
☐					
☐					
☐					
☐					
☐					
☐					
☐					
☐					
☐					
		TOTAL			

NOTES

MONTH ....

MONTHLY BILL TRACKER

YEAR ....

PAID	BILL	DUE DATE	AMOUNT DUE	AMOUNT PAID	UNPAID BALANCE
☐					
☐					
☐					
☐					
☐					
☐					
☐					
☐					
☐					
☐					
☐					
☐					
☐					
☐					
☐					
☐					
☐					
☐					
☐					
☐					
☐					
☐					
☐					
☐					
☐					
☐					
☐					
		TOTAL			

NOTES

MONTH

MONTHLY BILL TRACKER

YEAR

PAID	BILL	DUE DATE	AMOUNT DUE	AMOUNT PAID	UNPAID BALANCE
☐					
☐					
☐					
☐					
☐					
☐					
☐					
☐					
☐					
☐					
☐					
☐					
☐					
☐					
☐					
☐					
☐					
☐					
☐					
☐					
☐					
☐					
☐					
☐					
☐					
☐					
☐					
		TOTAL			

NOTES

MONTH

MONTHLY BILL TRACKER

YEAR

PAID	BILL	DUE DATE	AMOUNT DUE	AMOUNT PAID	UNPAID BALANCE
☐					
☐					
☐					
☐					
☐					
☐					
☐					
☐					
☐					
☐					
☐					
☐					
☐					
☐					
☐					
☐					
☐					
☐					
☐					
☐					
☐					
☐					
☐					
☐					
☐					
☐					
		TOTAL			

NOTES

MONTH

MONTHLY BILL TRACKER

YEAR

PAID	BILL	DUE DATE	AMOUNT DUE	AMOUNT PAID	UNPAID BALANCE
☐					
☐					
☐					
☐					
☐					
☐					
☐					
☐					
☐					
☐					
☐					
☐					
☐					
☐					
☐					
☐					
☐					
☐					
☐					
☐					
☐					
☐					
☐					
☐					
☐					
☐					
☐					
		TOTAL			

NOTES

MONTH

MONTHLY BILL TRACKER

YEAR

PAID	BILL	DUE DATE	AMOUNT DUE	AMOUNT PAID	UNPAID BALANCE
☐					
☐					
☐					
☐					
☐					
☐					
☐					
☐					
☐					
☐					
☐					
☐					
☐					
☐					
☐					
☐					
☐					
☐					
☐					
☐					
☐					
☐					
☐					
☐					
☐					
☐					
☐					
		TOTAL			

NOTES

MONTH

MONTHLY BILL TRACKER

YEAR

PAID	BILL	DUE DATE	AMOUNT DUE	AMOUNT PAID	UNPAID BALANCE
☐					
☐					
☐					
☐					
☐					
☐					
☐					
☐					
☐					
☐					
☐					
☐					
☐					
☐					
☐					
☐					
☐					
☐					
☐					
☐					
☐					
☐					
☐					
☐					
☐					
☐					
☐					
		TOTAL			

NOTES

MONTH ....

MONTHLY BILL TRACKER

YEAR ....

PAID	BILL	DUE DATE	AMOUNT DUE	AMOUNT PAID	UNPAID BALANCE
☐					
☐					
☐					
☐					
☐					
☐					
☐					
☐					
☐					
☐					
☐					
☐					
☐					
☐					
☐					
☐					
☐					
☐					
☐					
☐					
☐					
☐					
☐					
☐					
☐					
☐					
☐					
		TOTAL			

NOTES

....

....

....

MONTH

MONTHLY BILL TRACKER

YEAR

PAID	BILL	DUE DATE	AMOUNT DUE	AMOUNT PAID	UNPAID BALANCE
☐					
☐					
☐					
☐					
☐					
☐					
☐					
☐					
☐					
☐					
☐					
☐					
☐					
☐					
☐					
☐					
☐					
☐					
☐					
☐					
☐					
☐					
☐					
☐					
☐					
☐					
☐					
		TOTAL			

NOTES

MONTH

MONTHLY BILL TRACKER

YEAR

PAID	BILL	DUE DATE	AMOUNT DUE	AMOUNT PAID	UNPAID BALANCE
☐					
☐					
☐					
☐					
☐					
☐					
☐					
☐					
☐					
☐					
☐					
☐					
☐					
☐					
☐					
☐					
☐					
☐					
☐					
☐					
☐					
☐					
☐					
☐					
☐					
☐					
☐					
		TOTAL			

NOTES

MONTH ....

MONTHLY BILL TRACKER

YEAR ....

PAID	BILL	DUE DATE	AMOUNT DUE	AMOUNT PAID	UNPAID BALANCE
☐					
☐					
☐					
☐					
☐					
☐					
☐					
☐					
☐					
☐					
☐					
☐					
☐					
☐					
☐					
☐					
☐					
☐					
☐					
☐					
☐					
☐					
☐					
☐					
☐					
☐					
☐					
		TOTAL			

NOTES

MONTH

MONTHLY BILL TRACKER

YEAR

PAID	BILL	DUE DATE	AMOUNT DUE	AMOUNT PAID	UNPAID BALANCE
☐					
☐					
☐					
☐					
☐					
☐					
☐					
☐					
☐					
☐					
☐					
☐					
☐					
☐					
☐					
☐					
☐					
☐					
☐					
☐					
☐					
☐					
☐					
☐					
☐					
☐					
☐					
		TOTAL			

NOTES

MONTH

MONTHLY BILL TRACKER

YEAR

PAID	BILL	DUE DATE	AMOUNT DUE	AMOUNT PAID	UNPAID BALANCE
☐					
☐					
☐					
☐					
☐					
☐					
☐					
☐					
☐					
☐					
☐					
☐					
☐					
☐					
☐					
☐					
☐					
☐					
☐					
☐					
☐					
☐					
☐					
☐					
☐					
☐					
☐					
		TOTAL			

NOTES

MONTH

MONTHLY BILL TRACKER

YEAR

PAID	BILL	DUE DATE	AMOUNT DUE	AMOUNT PAID	UNPAID BALANCE
☐					
☐					
☐					
☐					
☐					
☐					
☐					
☐					
☐					
☐					
☐					
☐					
☐					
☐					
☐					
☐					
☐					
☐					
☐					
☐					
☐					
☐					
☐					
☐					
☐					
☐					
☐					
		TOTAL			

NOTES

MONTH

MONTHLY BILL TRACKER

YEAR

PAID	BILL	DUE DATE	AMOUNT DUE	AMOUNT PAID	UNPAID BALANCE
☐					
☐					
☐					
☐					
☐					
☐					
☐					
☐					
☐					
☐					
☐					
☐					
☐					
☐					
☐					
☐					
☐					
☐					
☐					
☐					
☐					
☐					
☐					
☐					
☐					
☐					
		TOTAL			

NOTES

MONTH

MONTHLY BILL TRACKER

YEAR

PAID	BILL	DUE DATE	AMOUNT DUE	AMOUNT PAID	UNPAID BALANCE
☐					
☐					
☐					
☐					
☐					
☐					
☐					
☐					
☐					
☐					
☐					
☐					
☐					
☐					
☐					
☐					
☐					
☐					
☐					
☐					
☐					
☐					
☐					
☐					
☐					
☐					
☐					
		TOTAL			

NOTES

MONTH ....

MONTHLY BILL TRACKER

YEAR ....

PAID	BILL	DUE DATE	AMOUNT DUE	AMOUNT PAID	UNPAID BALANCE
☐					
☐					
☐					
☐					
☐					
☐					
☐					
☐					
☐					
☐					
☐					
☐					
☐					
☐					
☐					
☐					
☐					
☐					
☐					
☐					
☐					
☐					
☐					
☐					
☐					
☐					
☐					
		TOTAL			

NOTES

MONTH

MONTHLY BILL TRACKER

YEAR

PAID	BILL	DUE DATE	AMOUNT DUE	AMOUNT PAID	UNPAID BALANCE
☐					
☐					
☐					
☐					
☐					
☐					
☐					
☐					
☐					
☐					
☐					
☐					
☐					
☐					
☐					
☐					
☐					
☐					
☐					
☐					
☐					
☐					
☐					
☐					
☐					
☐					
☐					
		TOTAL			

NOTES

MONTH ....

MONTHLY BILL TRACKER

YEAR ....

PAID	BILL	DUE DATE	AMOUNT DUE	AMOUNT PAID	UNPAID BALANCE
☐					
☐					
☐					
☐					
☐					
☐					
☐					
☐					
☐					
☐					
☐					
☐					
☐					
☐					
☐					
☐					
☐					
☐					
☐					
☐					
☐					
☐					
☐					
☐					
☐					
☐					
☐					
		TOTAL			

NOTES

MONTH

MONTHLY BILL TRACKER

YEAR

PAID	BILL	DUE DATE	AMOUNT DUE	AMOUNT PAID	UNPAID BALANCE
☐					
☐					
☐					
☐					
☐					
☐					
☐					
☐					
☐					
☐					
☐					
☐					
☐					
☐					
☐					
☐					
☐					
☐					
☐					
☐					
☐					
☐					
☐					
☐					
☐					
☐					
☐					
		TOTAL			

NOTES

MONTH

MONTHLY BILL TRACKER

YEAR

PAID	BILL	DUE DATE	AMOUNT DUE	AMOUNT PAID	UNPAID BALANCE
☐					
☐					
☐					
☐					
☐					
☐					
☐					
☐					
☐					
☐					
☐					
☐					
☐					
☐					
☐					
☐					
☐					
☐					
☐					
☐					
☐					
☐					
☐					
☐					
☐					
☐					
☐					
		TOTAL			

NOTES

MONTH

MONTHLY BILL TRACKER

YEAR

PAID	BILL	DUE DATE	AMOUNT DUE	AMOUNT PAID	UNPAID BALANCE
☐					
☐					
☐					
☐					
☐					
☐					
☐					
☐					
☐					
☐					
☐					
☐					
☐					
☐					
☐					
☐					
☐					
☐					
☐					
☐					
☐					
☐					
☐					
☐					
☐					
☐					
☐					
		TOTAL			

NOTES

MONTH ....

MONTHLY BILL TRACKER

YEAR ....

PAID	BILL	DUE DATE	AMOUNT DUE	AMOUNT PAID	UNPAID BALANCE
☐					
☐					
☐					
☐					
☐					
☐					
☐					
☐					
☐					
☐					
☐					
☐					
☐					
☐					
☐					
☐					
☐					
☐					
☐					
☐					
☐					
☐					
☐					
☐					
☐					
☐					
☐					
		TOTAL			

NOTES

....

....

....

MONTH ....

MONTHLY BILL TRACKER

YEAR ....

PAID	BILL	DUE DATE	AMOUNT DUE	AMOUNT PAID	UNPAID BALANCE
☐					
☐					
☐					
☐					
☐					
☐					
☐					
☐					
☐					
☐					
☐					
☐					
☐					
☐					
☐					
☐					
☐					
☐					
☐					
☐					
☐					
☐					
☐					
☐					
☐					
☐					
		TOTAL			

NOTES

....

....

....

MONTH

MONTHLY BILL TRACKER

YEAR

PAID	BILL	DUE DATE	AMOUNT DUE	AMOUNT PAID	UNPAID BALANCE
☐					
☐					
☐					
☐					
☐					
☐					
☐					
☐					
☐					
☐					
☐					
☐					
☐					
☐					
☐					
☐					
☐					
☐					
☐					
☐					
☐					
☐					
☐					
☐					
☐					
☐					
☐					
		TOTAL			

NOTES

MONTH

MONTHLY BILL TRACKER

YEAR

PAID	BILL	DUE DATE	AMOUNT DUE	AMOUNT PAID	UNPAID BALANCE
☐					
☐					
☐					
☐					
☐					
☐					
☐					
☐					
☐					
☐					
☐					
☐					
☐					
☐					
☐					
☐					
☐					
☐					
☐					
☐					
☐					
☐					
☐					
☐					
☐					
☐					
☐					
		TOTAL			

NOTES

MONTH

MONTHLY BILL TRACKER

YEAR

PAID	BILL	DUE DATE	AMOUNT DUE	AMOUNT PAID	UNPAID BALANCE
☐					
☐					
☐					
☐					
☐					
☐					
☐					
☐					
☐					
☐					
☐					
☐					
☐					
☐					
☐					
☐					
☐					
☐					
☐					
☐					
☐					
☐					
☐					
☐					
☐					
☐					
☐					
		TOTAL			

NOTES

MONTH

MONTHLY BILL TRACKER

YEAR

PAID	BILL	DUE DATE	AMOUNT DUE	AMOUNT PAID	UNPAID BALANCE
☐					
☐					
☐					
☐					
☐					
☐					
☐					
☐					
☐					
☐					
☐					
☐					
☐					
☐					
☐					
☐					
☐					
☐					
☐					
☐					
☐					
☐					
☐					
☐					
☐					
☐					
☐					
		TOTAL			

NOTES